How To...

AUDIO ACCESS INCLUDED

PLAY BLUES/ROCK GUITAR SOLOS

By David Grissom

PLAYBACK+
Speed • Pitch • Balance • Loop

To access audio visit:
www.halleonard.com/mylibrary

Enter Code
3283-6936-0773-4348

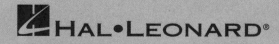

7777 W. BLUEMOUND RD. P.O. BOX 13819 MILWAUKEE, WI 53213

ISBN 978-1-5400-0548-9

In Australia Contact:
Hal Leonard Australia Pty. Ltd.
4 Lentara Court
Cheltenham, Victoria, 3192 Australia
Email: ausadmin@halleonard.com.au

Visit Hal Leonard Online at
www.halleonard.com

ABOUT THE AUTHOR

David Grissom has toured and recorded with such artists as John Mellencamp, Joe Ely, Storyville, the Allman Brothers Band, Chris Isaak, Robben Ford, the Fabulous Thunderbirds, Montgomery Gentry, Ringo Starr, Buddy Guy, John Mayall, Martina McBride, and Jennifer Warnes. His songs have been recorded by Trisha Yearwood, John Mayall, Lee Ann Womack, Shannon Curfman, and Storyville, among others. He has been featured several times in *Guitar Player*, *Guitar World*, *Musician*, and *Vintage Guitar* magazines.

EQUIPMENT AND GEAR NOTES

On the audio tracks, I play a Paul Reed Smith McCarty model through a '71 Marshall 20-watt head into a '69 4x12 cabinet. Occasionally, I use a little delay and overdrive—nothing fancy. On my PRSs, I use D'Addario strings gauged .011 through .049. On Fenders, I use a .010-.046 set. Unless you are playing all of the time, I don't recommend using anything heavier than .010 to .046 if you want to do much string bending.

I have two different pedalboards; I keep one for studio work and then a smaller one for live playing. The smaller one fits into a small anvil briefcase. I used to carry all of my pedals loose in a gym bag and plug them in as needed. It took me 15 years to figure out that it is a whole lot easier to have everything permanently mounted on a board. Both of my pedalboards have a tuner, a Klon Centaur overdrive, a Line 6 delay, an Arion chorus/flanger, and a tremolo pedal. The bigger board has a volume pedal and some empty slots in which I'm always trying out new pedals.

Finding the gear that is right for you is a matter of experimenting. Have fun and good luck!

ACKNOWLEDGMENTS

Thanks to Paul Smith and everyone at PRS Guitars, D'Addario strings and Planet Waves cables, Jerry Jones Guitars, Marshall Amplification, Dr. Z Amplification, Mark Sampson, Hamer Guitars, Jeff Bowen and Fender Musical Instruments, Line 6, and Collings Guitars.

This book is dedicated to my guitar teachers, Philip Franchini, Jeff Sherman, and Sam Todd. Thank you for your gifts of inspiration and knowledge.

CONTENTS

INTRODUCTION

"Do you play rhythm or lead?"

I must have been asked that question a thousand times. While I find it somewhat humorous that so many people assume you can play "lead" without having an understanding of rhythm guitar, I think it indicates that "lead," or *soloing*, is where it's at for most people. While playing rhythm is an art unto itself, to the average listener, soloing is what really sets the great players apart. In as little as a few bars, the right solo can make a great song even better. How we approach soloing stamps out our identities as players—I can usually identify my favorite soloists within a few notes.

As you'll see in this book, soloing is not only a function of our influences and training, but of our personalities as well. How a player combines these elements along with tone is what distinguishes one player from the next—the good from the great.

Whether I'm carving a five-minute solo with the Allman Brothers or a four-bar solo with John Mellencamp, my goal is always to play with soul and emotion. Over the years my approach to soloing has become more one of "feel" where I let the vibe of the song and what is going on around me influence what I play. There were many steps and enlightening moments along the way that brought me to this point. This is what this book is about.

Enough talk. Let's rock!

 Track 73

Note: Track 73 contains tuning notes (low E to high E) for your reference.

CHAPTER 1
TWO THINGS YOU MUST KNOW

I've played guitar for 40 years, and I've found that there aren't a lot of shortcuts when it comes to growing as a guitarist. There is no substitute for hours spent playing your instrument. There are, however, two absolutes which can help you to focus and learn faster.

First, you must *learn where the notes are on the fingerboard*. Whenever I give a clinic, I always ask how many people can locate all of the notes on the neck. I'm always surprised at how few people raise their hands. I promise that it will make your life much simpler, and learning to play guitar a lot more fun, if you can learn this one thing. I was fortunate to have a teacher who stressed this from the beginning. Here's a fretboard diagram to help you on your way.

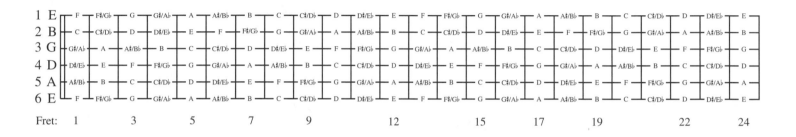

Start by mastering the high and low E strings—they contain the same notes in different octaves. Next, learn the notes on the 5th string—you'll be able to begin practicing scales, and you'll know where the roots of power chords are to be found. When you become comfortable, learn the other three strings. Note that at the 12th fret, the notes of each string start repeating an octave higher. The goal is to become fluent enough so that you don't have to think "technical thoughts." It is hard to be in the zone on a B♭ blues if you don't know where the B♭s are.

The second thing you must know is that the tone is in your hands. That is, the sound that comes out of the amplifier is mainly the result of how you touch the strings. Yes, equipment is important, but ultimately it is whether you use a pick or the flesh of your hand, the pressure you use to fret and pick, and every other nuance of touch that determines tone. Check out the example below. On the left channel the sound is from the amplifier, and on the right it is from a microphone placed next to the strings. Pan back and forth to understand how the tone really is in your hands.

 Track 1

CHAPTER 2
WHAT MAKES A GREAT SOLO?

Think of your favorite solos—what is it about each of them that makes them stand out? Is it the player's technique, his tone, the notes he plays, the emotion you feel, or the way the solo builds? Chances are it is a combination of all these things. Melody, dynamics, and phrasing are all elements that define a solo.

Melody concerns the actual notes that are played. Sometimes it works great for a solo just to reprise or embellish the basic melody of a song. For instance, if the solo is played over the same chords as the chorus of a song, you could just play the vocal melody instrumentally. Countless classic solos (many Beatles solos, for instance) are based on the melody of a tune. Jeff Beck is a master at starting with the melody of a song and building intensity as he improvises variations on the melody. Check out "Cause We've Ended as Lovers" or "Goodbye Pork Pie Hat" for good examples of this (as well as everything else discussed in this chapter). There are also great solos that rely less on melody than they do on rhythm and raw emotion. Most of the solos you'll find on a Rage Against the Machine album, as well as many classic two- or three-note blues solos, are good examples of this.

Dynamics refers to how loudly or softly one plays. Sometimes it is appropriate to blaze through a solo at full volume the whole way. Other times it can be more effective to start quietly and build to the very end. Of course, like other elements that define a solo, there are no set rules.

Phrasing refers to the rhythmic groupings of notes. There are an infinite number of possibilities regarding how to phrase a solo, even if you are using only a few notes and have only a couple of bars to play over.

When playing a solo, my first priority is the song. How can the solo enhance or even improve the song? What do the lyrics say? Unless irony is your goal, you probably don't want to play a million notes through a Marshall at "11" over a sappy love song. You probably wouldn't be inclined to play a gorgeous melody over a hardcore funk groove (or would you?). Soloing is very much like a conversation except that you are talking with your guitar. When you are telling someone you love them, you use a certain tone of voice. When you are angry about something, you probably speak more loudly and use a whole different set of words to get your point across.

My favorite solos always affect me on an emotional level. They might rip my heart out with their beauty or knock me over with their power, but either way, it is emotion and soul that I'm always looking for.

CHAPTER 3
RULE NUMBER ONE

Rule Number One is: You can always play 1. That is, once you know what key you're in, you can always play the tonic. What this means is that you can start playing solos *right now*. The all-important point is that you must know where that note is on the neck. Better yet, you should know *all* of the places on the neck where you can play that note.

The following example illustrates what you can do with just one note. I solo here by playing A at different places on the neck. Because I limit myself to one note, I create interest by varying the rhythm and dynamics. Sometimes I bend into the note, and a few times I add the E just below.

Dial up a fat tone and go!

 Track 2

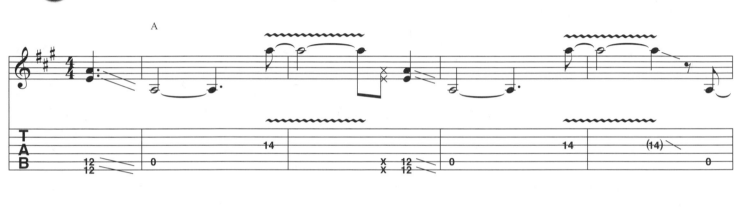

CHAPTER 4
SCALES

Scales are the language of music and the foundation for improvising a solo. Just as we choose words to make a sentence and convey a thought, a scale is a group of notes that, when played together, defines a musical tonality. By learning and practicing scales, you will develop fluency on the fingerboard and teach your ear to recognize the right notes to play over any given set of chord changes.

For the most part, rock music is *modal* (as explained below). When you determine the key of the song and whether it is major or minor, you have the liberty of soloing on that one scale if you desire. If you are playing over more advanced chord changes, you will most likely use many different scales in that one song. Most great players rarely play a straight scale in a solo. They may use a particular scale as a launching point, but they usually choose and mix notes in an imaginative and musical way. The ultimate goal is to not have to think about which scale to play, but rather to let your ear be the guide.

The Major Scale

Let's look first at the *major scale*. While it is not very often that you would use a straight major scale in a typical blues-based rock song, this scale is necessary to understanding basic music theory. Each note of the scale has a corresponding number. For instance, a C major scale is C–D–E–F–G–A–B; C is "1," D is "2," E is "3," F is "4," G is "5," A is "6," and B is "7." Throughout the book, I refer to numbers based on the major scale. For instance, if we are in the key of G (by the way, the G major scale is G–A–B–C–D–E–F♯), and I refer to the "flat 7," I'm talking about F♮.

The major scale has seven corresponding *modes*. All of these modes contain the same notes as the major scale, but start on different degrees of the scale. For instance, if you play the notes of the C major scale but start on 2 (D), this is known as the Dorian mode (D–E–F–G–A–B–C), or, more precisely, "D Dorian." "C Dorian" means you would start on the note C and play the notes of the major scale of which C is the second degree (in other words, you'd play a B♭ major scale starting on C).

The modes are:

Ionian (starts on 1)

Dorian (starts on 2)

Phrygian (starts on 3)

Lydian (starts on 4)

Mixolydian (starts on 5)

Aeolian (starts on 6)

Locrian (starts on 7)

The most common modes I use are Mixolydian and Dorian. G Mixolydian contains the notes of the C major scale starting on G; D Dorian contains the notes of the C major scale starting on D. So while you may not always use a straight C major scale while playing in C, knowing the fingering for a major scale is *extremely important* because you'll need the skill for playing modes.

The two basic fingerings for the major scale are:

Root on 6th String (G Major)

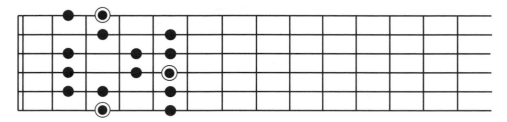

Root on 5th String (D Major)

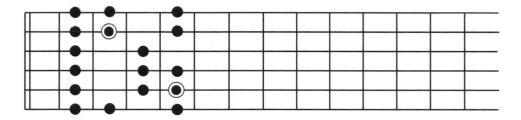

The circled notes indicate the tonic. Finger the notes following the standard "one finger for each fret" method, and note that these fingerings are movable! So, if you learn the basic fingering for the G major scale starting on the 6th string, you'll also know how to play any other major scale by moving the fretting pattern around the neck. For instance, to play an A major scale, move the same fingering up two frets; to play the C major scale, move up five frets. Now compare the C major scale starting on the 8th fret (6th string) with the C major fingering starting on the 3rd fret (5th string). See if you can find a fingering that connects the two. Ultimately, you want to be fluent up and down the neck so you're not limited to just one or two positions.

The Blues Scale

The *blues scale,* as its name implies, is used over blues-based chord progressions. You can use this scale in most blues tunes as well as in any song that has a solo section over one chord. The blues scale is 1–♭3–4–♭5–5–♭7. In G, this translates to G–B♭–C–D♭–D–F♮.

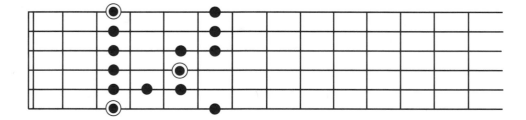

Pentatonic Scales

Pentatonic scales are five-note scales that I use all the time. The major pentatonic scale is 1–2–3–5–6. G pentatonic is G–A–B–D–E.

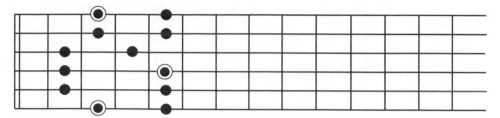

The minor pentatonic scale is 1–♭3–4–5–♭7. G minor pentatonic is G–B♭–C–D–F♮.

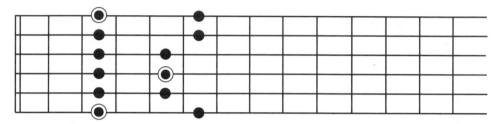

Notice that the minor pentatonic scale is the same thing as the blues scale, but without the ♭5.

The Chromatic Scale

The chromatic scale is literally every note. Very rarely do I play a chromatic scale for any length of time. Rather, chromatic notes are used as passing tones within other scales. When it comes to passing tones, there really aren't any "wrong" notes. Because they occur only "in passing," anything goes; this is where you can throw the rules out the window. Use your ears—does it sound good to you? When I'm soloing over a minor progression, I sometimes use the major 3rd as a passing tone. The ♭2, ♭5, and ♭7 are commonly used as passing tones in a variety of situations and provide welcome relief to using a straight scale all the time. Check out the next example. I play a B chord without a 3rd on the rhythm track; I mix chromatics in with other scales. As I said, anything goes.

 Track 3

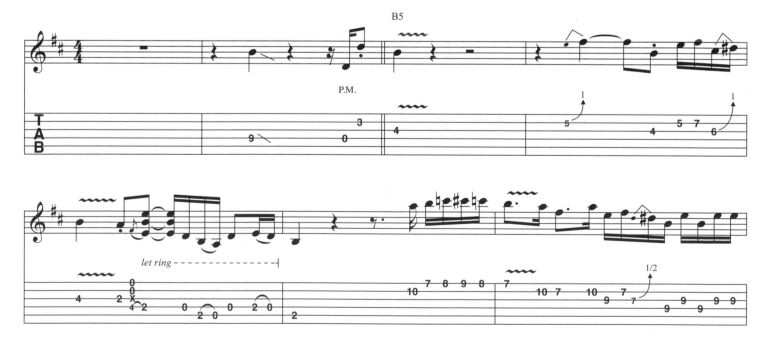

While it is easy to get bogged down and frustrated with scales, there are many situations in rock soloing where there really aren't any wrong notes. I'll take a "wrong note" with attitude any day over a lame solo with nothing but so-called "right" notes.

I encourage you to learn as much as possible about scales and modes. I also encourage you to experiment. Listen to all kinds of music and mix it up. Steal ideas from everywhere and make them your own. Learning to play guitar is like putting together a puzzle or learning to ride a bike. For all of the hours of hard work and frustration, there are moments of illumination when things make sense and fall in to place. This is especially true of learning scales and basic theory.

CHAPTER 5
PICKING TECHNIQUES

How you choose to strike the strings with your right hand has as much to do with tone as the guitar and amp you choose to play. On one end of the spectrum, some players use a pick to play every note. On the other end, there are players who don't use a pick at all but use their fingers exclusively. There are advantages to both techniques. I prefer a hybrid style that uses both a pick and the 2nd and 3rd fingers of my right hand. I think this approach combines the best of both worlds. There are some sounds you can get only with a pick and others you can get only with your bare fingers. I encourage you to experiment with different approaches to picking and find out what works best for you. There really is no right or wrong here.

When I first started playing I gradually developed a picking style that involved playing a downstroke whenever I went to a new string. I didn't consciously do this—it was just what felt natural to me. When I began taking lessons shortly thereafter, my teacher told me that this was wrong and that I should always use alternate picking no matter what—that is, always alternate up and down strokes. I've found that there are advantages to both methods, but I have gradually found myself going back to my original instincts lately. The point is that if a particular technique seems to work well for you, then go for it. The most unique and original players have always broken the rules when it comes to technique.

Practicing scales is a great way to develop dexterity and experiment with different methods of picking. Practice playing major scales in different positions on the neck, first with all downstrokes and then using alternate picking. Practicing both ways will help you to improve more quickly. When you do this, go only as quickly as you can play cleanly. This may be excruciatingly slow at first, but the last thing you want to do is learn bad habits. Take your time and be patient.

Let's look more closely at the hybrid style I mentioned earlier. I hold the pick with my thumb and 1st finger and use my 2nd and 3rd fingers as needed. One of the techniques I use a lot is to "pop" a string. I literally grab the string with my 3rd finger and let it snap back on the neck. In the next example, I pop all but the sixth note, which I strike with the pick.

Track 4

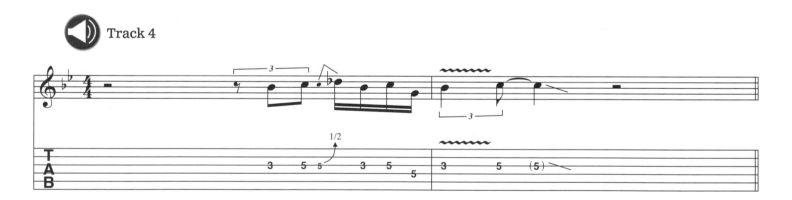

This technique produces a really aggressive sound that can't be duplicated any other way. Blues greats Albert Collins, Albert King, and Stevie Ray Vaughan used this technique a lot. The next example is played entirely with my middle finger popping the notes. I play over A minor here.

 **Track 5**

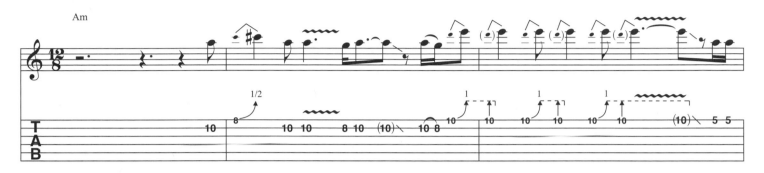

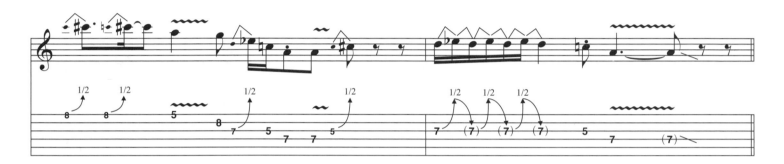

Another technique I use a lot is to *pedal* a note (essentially, repeat it under or over a melody line) with my pick on the 4th string and use my 2nd and 3rd fingers to strike the 3rd and 2nd strings, respectively. I pedal the 4th string with alternate picking, but I always play a downstroke before I strike the note(s) with my fingers. In this example, I play an A with the 1st finger of my left hand. When I play the E and G, I use my 3rd and 2nd fingers, respectively. When I play the D and F♯, I barre with my 1st finger. I play off an A Mixolydian scale here.

 **Track 6**

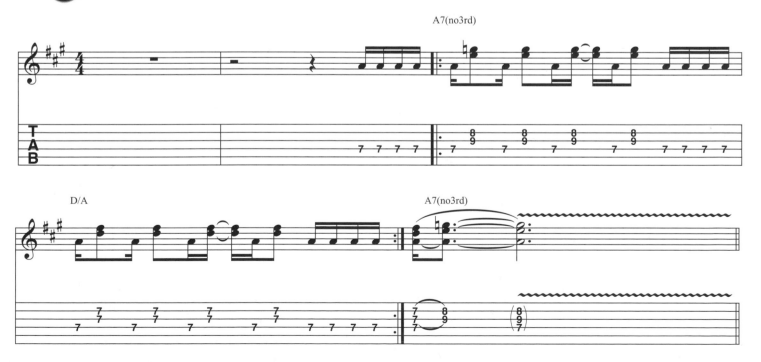

Sometimes I'll play all downstrokes on the 4th string. Here I elaborate on the previous example by playing a more complex rhythm and playing some higher notes on the 1st string. As before, I play off an A Mixolydian scale, which can also be thought of as a D major scale starting on A.

 Track 7

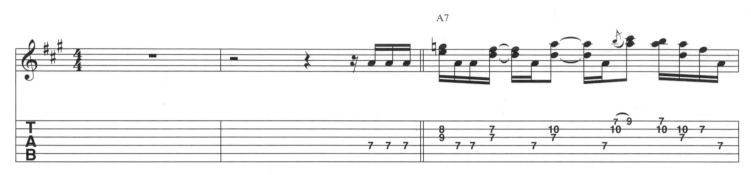

When you get comfortable with this technique, you can do the double time thing.

 **Track 8**

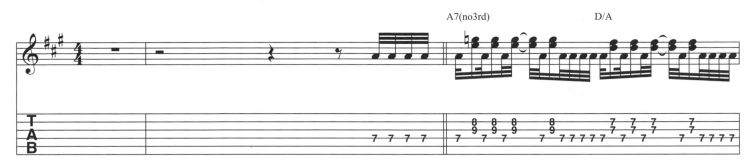

One cool sound that you can get only with a pick is an *artificial harmonic*—a very fancy name for a very raunchy sound. If you've ever heard ZZ Top's Billy Gibbons, you know what I'm talkin' about. The key to this sound is to have plenty of overdrive dialed in on your amp, or to use some kind of overdrive/distortion pedal. Hold your pick so that just after the pick strikes the string your thumb touches it, creating the harmonic. Check it out.

I start with my 3rd finger (left hand) playing A on the 4th string (7th fret). For maximum squawk, use your bridge pickup and experiment with where you actually pick (closer to and farther away from the bridge). You also might find that muting with the heel of your right hand helps; let it rest lightly on the bridge, muting just enough to keep the strings you are not picking from ringing.

Track 9

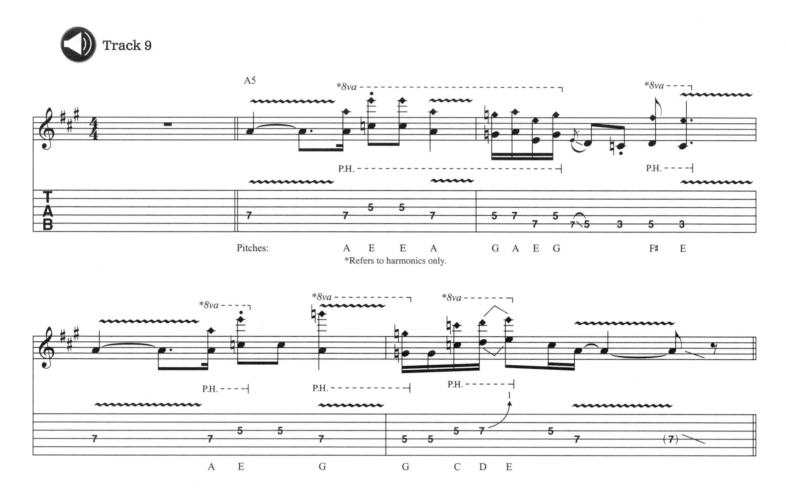

Finding the picking style that works for you is a matter of experimentation. Practice!

CHAPTER 6

STRING BENDING AND OTHER LEFT-HAND TECHNIQUES

String bending, vibrato, pull-offs, and hammer-ons are all fundamental techniques in rock soloing. Combining these basic left-hand techniques with a variety of picking techniques will allow you to make the most of your guitar's unique personality and will provide you with countless ways to play a lick. Unlike other instruments such as the piano, the guitar's unique properties allow you to play the same note at different places on the neck. While this makes reading music for guitar more complicated, it also allows for a greater variety of timbral choices and fingering possibilities. Most importantly, the fact that you can bend around or in between notes provides a very powerful tool of expression.

When I bend strings, I most commonly fret the note I'm bending with my 3rd finger and push the string towards the ceiling to bend it (as opposed to pulling down). I place my 1st and 2nd fingers on the string as well to provide support for the 3rd finger. I usually have my left thumb over the neck (and sometimes on the fingerboard either muting strings or fretting a note) to provide as much leverage as possible. I often use the other fingers of my left hand to bend, but right now let's concentrate on the 3rd finger.

Here is a lick in A—bending with the 3rd finger on the 2nd string. Play this lick starting with the B bent up two frets to a C♯. If anything, I bend just shy of the C♯. In fact, I recommend that if you are not sure how far to bend, always err on the flat side of the note. It sounds cooler than bending sharp.

 Track 10

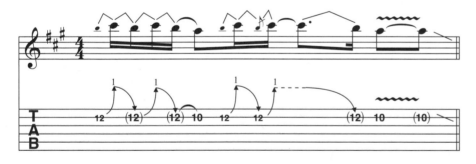

Here is a variation of the last lick. On the sixth note, bend up an extra fret to the D (still starting the bend on B).

 Track 11

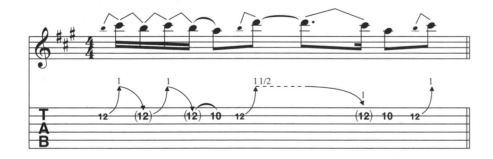

Now let's add some vibrato to the bend.

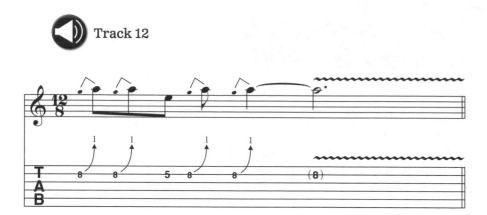

Track 12

Notice how I hold the last note using a slow vibrato. This gives the lick a soulful, vocal quality and makes the note sustain longer. Here is the same lick with a fast vibrato.

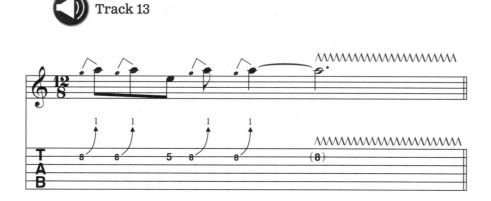

Track 13

Either way, make sure that your thumb is wrapped over the top of the neck and that you keep your 1st and 2nd fingers behind the 3rd to get as much support and strength as possible.

Of course, you don't have to bend a note to use vibrato. In the next example, I use my 3rd finger to get vibrato on both of the A notes.

Track 14

Sometimes I bend a note one fret with my 2nd finger . . .

Track 15

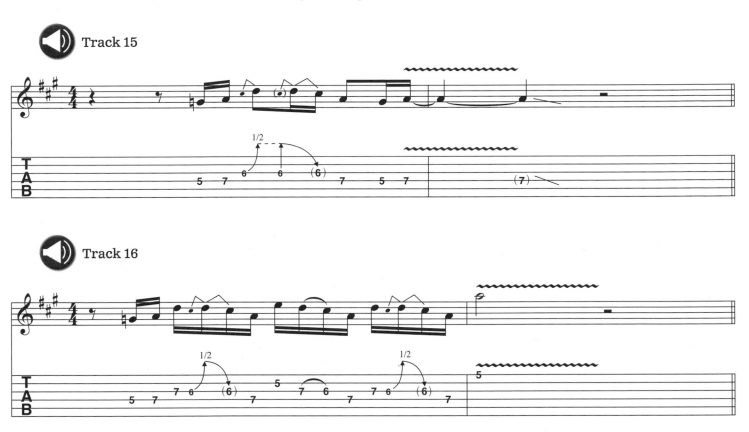

Track 16

. . . or my 1st finger.

Track 17

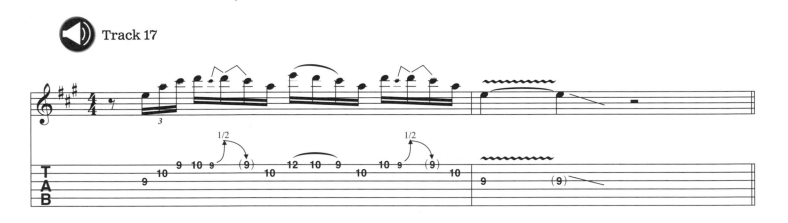

In the next example, I use my 1st finger to bend from the minor 3rd a little less than a fret. I bend just shy of the C♯—I use these "in between notes" all the time.

Track 18

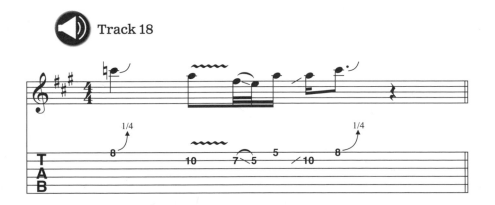

Pull-offs and *hammer-ons* are effects you can create with your left hand. Usually, you pick a note and then pull off or hammer on from that note with one of your left-hand fingers. A pull-off in its simplest form works like this: When the 3rd finger pulls off the E, it sounds the D (fretted with the 1st finger).

 Track 19

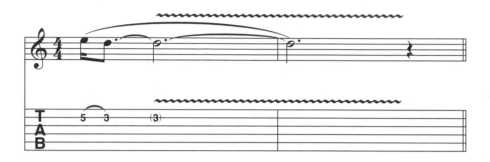

Here is a fancier example.

 Track 20

Here is a simple hammer-on. Pick the open D string and hammer on the E with the 2nd finger of your left hand.

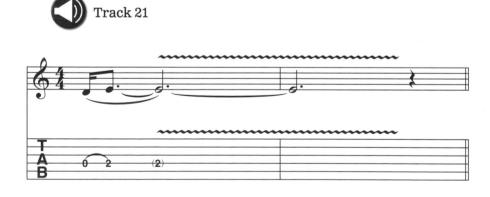 Track 21

Now try this one.

 Track 22

Here is a lick that combines pull-offs and hammer-ons.

 Track 23

Another technique I employ a lot is using my left thumb to fret notes or to mute the 5th and 6th strings. There are many licks and chord voicings that are impossible without using your thumb. In this example, I fret the A on the 6th string with my thumb. I use my pick to play the A and my middle finger to play the notes above it.

 Track 24

*Finger all 6th string notes w/ l.h. thumb.

Fretting with your thumb may seem difficult at first if you're not used to it, but once you get this technique under control it opens up a world of possibilities.

CHAPTER 7
IT ALL STARTS WITH THE BLUES

The foundation of rock soloing is the blues. Most of the great rock soloists of the last 30 years can trace their styles back to blues influences. Thousands of rock songs have been written using a standard 12-bar blues framework. The simplicity and emotion in a great blues solo is also a great place for us to start making some music. Let's begin with the blues scale in A. Here's a diagram of the fretting.

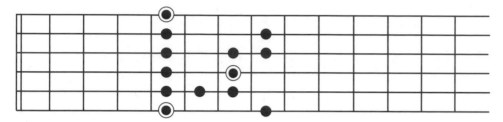

Play this scale below starting on A (the tonic) on the 5th fret of the 6th string. Try playing it with all downstrokes, and then with alternate picking. Go as slowly as you have to in order to play it cleanly. Practicing both picking methods will give your fingers a good workout and let you hear the different sounds of each method. On the track, I play this using all downstrokes, which to me sounds more aggressive.

Track 25

Now let's try a basic lick in A using the scale. It starts with your third finger at the 7th fret. When you get to the fourth note of this lick (E♭), notice that I bend into it from the previous note (D). I pick the E♭ just as I bend the string the appropriate length (half step). The next two notes are not actually picked—I let the string bend back down to D (still with my 3rd finger) and pull off my 3rd finger to make the C sound. I use downstrokes here. If you are just starting out, you can play this lick without any bends or the pull-off.

Now let's play a 12-bar blues solo based on this lick. In this example, I use the lick I played in the previous example as a *theme* or, if you want to get fancy, a *motif*. I took the basic idea and elaborated on it. This is a very common improvisation technique, used especially during long solos.

Track 27

*T = Thumb on 6th string

Some people are baffled by the concept of improvising. Think of improvising a solo as having a conversation with someone. If you are trying to make a point, you generally start by stating that point and then backing it up with other related statements—you generally don't start reeling off a lot of random, unrelated ideas. Improvising or playing a solo can be thought of in the same way. Practice taking a basic lick and building on it. You can do this over any set of chord changes. If you want someone to really listen to your solo, this is a way to draw them in and keep their interest.

In this next example, I play a 12-bar blues progression with the G blues scale. After a two-bar drum intro, I play through the changes twice. Each 12-bar cycle is called a *chorus*. Both times I use the first four bars of each chorus to state a theme on which I build in the next eight bars. Notice that in the second chorus I start with a higher group of notes to build intensity as the solo progresses.

Track 28

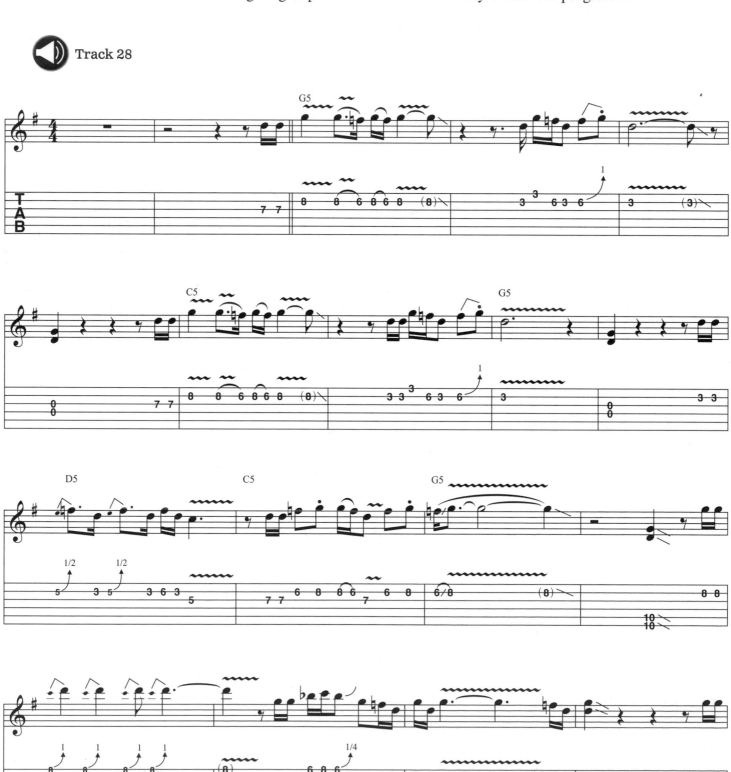

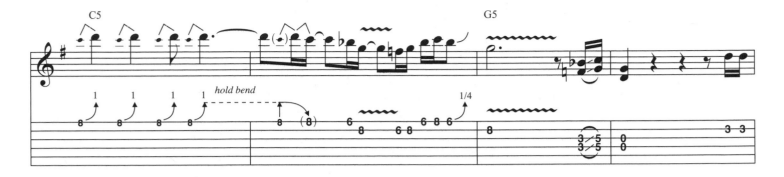

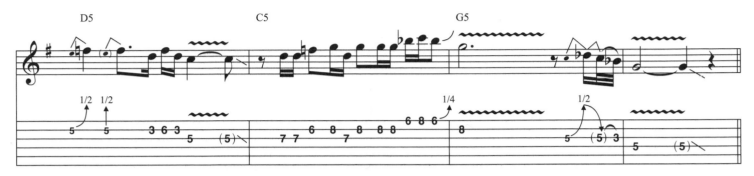

So far we've been soloing over blues changes using the blues and minor pentatonic scales. You've probably noticed that there is only a one-note difference between the two scales—the ♭5 in the blues scale. You also may have noticed that neither scale has a "normal" (i.e., major) 3 in it—both have a ♭3. Now let's take a look at a couple of scales that do have that major 3rd: the major pentatonic and the Mixolydian scales.

The major pentatonic scale (1–2–3–5–6) can be used in any situation where the tonality is major. Let's take a look at the fingering for the D pentatonic major scale.

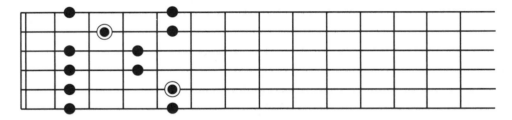

Here is a descending lick starting on the 2nd string, 3rd fret. Play the D with your second finger. When you get to the F♯ on the 4th string, fret it with your second finger as well, slide down to the E, and pull off to the D. Keep using your second finger to play the B and pull off to the A.

 Track 29 Slow and Fast Versions

Try this expanded version of the last lick, starting an octave higher. The first note is D on the 1st string, 10th fret.

Track 30 Slow and Fast Versions

Those last two licks have an Allman Brothers, almost country, vibe. The major pentatonic scale can also sound very bluesy . . .

Track 31

. . . or jazzy.

Track 32

The other scale commonly used in rock and blues that has a "normal" 3 is the Mixolydian scale. Take a look at the fingering for D Mixolydian.

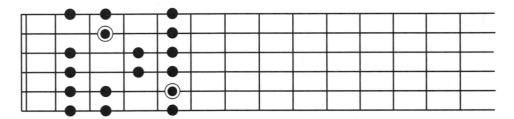

If you were to superimpose a G major scale over this diagram you would see that they contain the same notes. The Mixolydian scale has all of the notes of the major pentatonic scale as well as a 4 and a ♭7.

Track 33

In this next example, I vamp over D7 and improvise using the Mixolydian scale.

Track 34

If you are just learning how to solo and improvise, it can be confusing keeping track of all of these scales. Remember that ultimately you don't want to be bogged down with a lot of technical thoughts. When you get to a certain level of proficiency, you will be able to play "in the moment" and let your ear be your guide. Muscle memory also comes in to play. The more you practice scales, the more getting around the fingerboard becomes second nature—you actually train your muscles and eliminate some of the technical thought process. Here are some basic principles that can allow you to get past thinking strictly about individual scales.

The typical 12-bar blues consists of three chords: I, IV, and V. In the key of G, that translates to G, C, and D. In the most basic form of the blues, the chords are played as follows.

$\frac{4}{4}$ G |G |G |G |

      C |C |G |G |

      D |C |G |G ||

It is also very common to substitute a IV chord (here, C) in the second measure. Either way, a very general rule is to avoid playing the 3 of the key over the IV chord (think of this as Rule Number Two!). In G, this means to avoid playing a B note over the C chord—the B♭ sounds better. Of course, there are exceptions to this rule, especially if you are using the B as a passing tone. In most cases, however, this is a bulletproof shortcut. Check it out.

 **Track 35**

Just in case you don't believe me, here is the same set of chords. This time, I played the B over the IV chord. This makes my dog run howling from the room.

Track 36

You'll also notice that I avoid playing the B over the V chord. Don't worry—you'll find ways to break these rules but, in general, they will do you a lot of good.

When I solo over blues changes, I don't really think about scales. In fact, I draw on and move in and out of all of the scales we've discussed here. Other than avoiding playing the 3 over the IV chord, I don't think in technical terms. As long as I know what key I'm in, I'm cool. I know that I can always play the 1, and from there I know my way around the fingerboard. What I do think about is building the solo and playing with intensity. If it is a short solo, I might come in slamming and keep it that way. If it is a long solo, I try to give it someplace to go, building intensity along the way.

Initially I learned to play by copying solos off records; I encourage you to do the same. Your ear will develop more quickly, you'll get a better idea of how great players build their solos, and a lot of things that seem confusing early on will become more obvious along the way.

CHAPTER 8
USING OPEN STRINGS

As we said before, some of the things that make the guitar more difficult to play also give the instrument its unique personality. For instance, a D played on the 2nd string at the 3rd fret sounds subtly different than a D played on the 3rd string at the 7th fret, or the D played on the 4th string at the 10th fret. This is because of the difference in the sizes (*gauges*) of the strings and the point at which each note is fretted on the neck. One of the most unique things about the guitar is the seemingly infinite possibilities of combining open strings with fretted notes. To my ears, every key has a personality of its own. I'm sure there are some complicated psychoacoustic reasons for this, but I've come to believe that how the open strings relate to a given key is the main factor that gives each key its unique quality.

In certain keys, the use of open strings is pretty obvious. Here is a blues/pentatonic lick in E that uses all six open strings.

 Track 37   Fast and Slow Versions

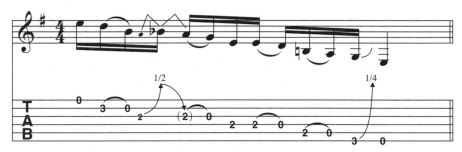

These 1st position licks are the easiest to learn and probably the most familiar to the majority of players. This lick is played on the top four strings with the 1st and 2nd fingers of the left hand.

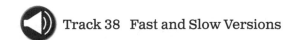 Track 38   Fast and Slow Versions

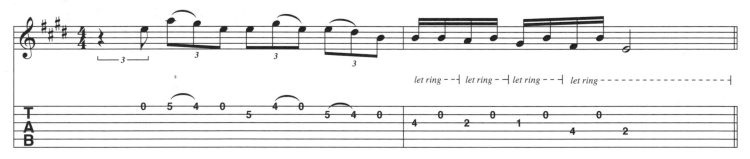

The bottom line is that if the key or scale you are playing in has an E, A, D, G, or B (the notes of the open strings), you can use that string in a lick or chord even if you are playing way up the neck. The possibilities are endless.

I like to take advantage of close intervals with open strings, which creates a little bit of dissonance and tension but sounds really musical to me, especially when used in passing. In this example, the G is played open on the third string against the F♯ on the 4th string and the open D string is played against the C♯ on the 5th string. Notice that in the second half of the lick the A fretted on the 6th string is followed by the open A.

 Track 39   Fast and Slow Versions

One of my favorite sounds is to use an open string note as a *drone* (a note that is held and/or repeated while other musical activity is going on) while I play a lick on another string. This example uses the open E string as a drone while the melody is played on the strings below it. In the first half of the lick, I use just the pick to play the melody on the 2nd string; in the second half of the lick, I use both pick and fingers so I can play notes below the 2nd string. I could also play the same melody and use the B string as a drone by playing the first half of the melody on the 3rd string if I wanted to.

 Track 40

B is one of my favorite keys because of its open string possibilities. Check out this blues lick that uses the open B string as a drone while also using the open D, A, and low E strings.

 Track 41

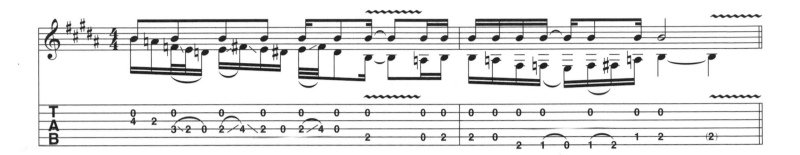

I love to use the open B and high E strings as well, especially over a major chord or Mixolydian scale.

 Track 42

Now, here is almost the same lick using the same scale over an F#m7. Technically, I'm playing in F# Dorian here (the second mode of the major scale). You could also think of this and the previous example as in E major. F# Dorian and B Mixolydian contain the same notes as the E major scale. I point this out to emphasize the importance of learning the major scale fingerings and to try and demystify modes for you.

 Track 43

G is another key that really lends itself to using open strings. All of the notes on the open strings are in the G scale. If you are playing in G minor, or are on the IV chord of a blues progression, just avoid the B string.

The same thing applies to A—there is no C# open string (the 3rd of A). You can pretty much use any open string at any time.

The only keys that aren't particularly "open-string friendly" (to me, at least) are A♭ and D♭, but there are worlds of possibilities in all of the other keys.

CHAPTER 9
DOUBLE STOPS

Playing two notes at the same time is called a *double stop*. Double stops are often used in country, blues, and R & B, and are a powerful tool in rock soloing. Here is a Chuck Berry–style lick starting on the 5th fret. Use your 1st finger to barre the notes on the 5th fret and your 3rd finger to barre the notes on the 7th and 8th frets.

Track 44   Fast and Slow Versions

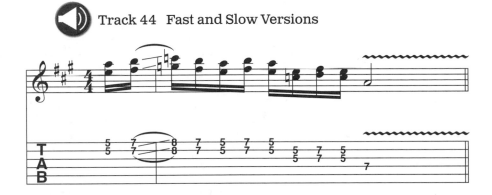

This lick starts with single notes, but then goes to double stops.

Track 45   Fast and Slow Versions

Now let's play some double stops with different fingerings. In the next example, play the top note with your 1st finger and the bottom note with either your 2nd or 3rd finger. Except for the last note, play the entire phrase on the 1st and 2nd strings

Track 46   Fast and Slow Versions

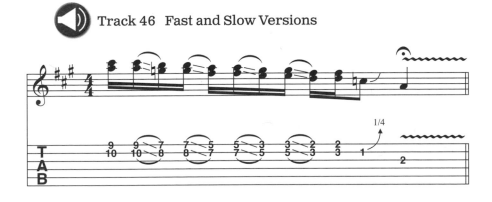

A technique I really like is to use one of the lower strings as a pedal tone while playing a double stop lick above it. In this example, I pick the open A string for the pedal tone and use my 2nd and 3rd fingers to play the 4th and 3rd strings, respectively.

 Track 47

Now try bending one of the strings in a double stop. In this example, I bend the 3rd string with my 3rd finger and play the top note with my 4th finger on the 2nd string.

Track 48

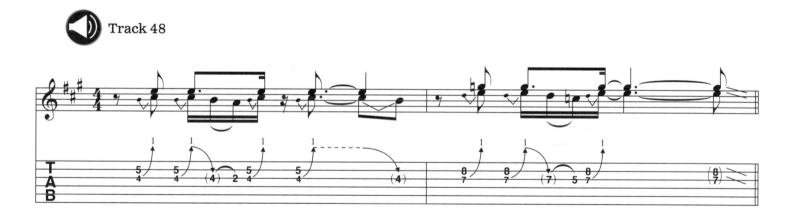

Except for the last notes, I play the next lick on the 1st and 2nd strings.

Track 49   Fast and Slow Versions

Now let's combine straight double stops with bent strings. I like to play this type of lick using the 2nd and 3rd fingers of my right hand, but you can certainly use a pick if you want. If you do use a pick, try using all downstrokes to give it a more aggressive sound.

Track 50

Let's now look at some more R & B–based approaches to soloing. To get this tone, use the neck pickup on your guitar and play all downstrokes. I play the first half of this lick starting in 9th position (my 1st finger is at the 9th fret) and the second half in 7th position; I finish the lick with an A and a C♯ on the 4th and 3rd strings. You can also play this lick starting in 5th position and ending in 2nd position, but I think it sounds warmer to play this type of lick in the middle of the neck and fingerboard as much as possible.

Track 51   Fast and Slow Versions

In the next example you could play the first lick on the top two strings but, once again, I think it sounds fatter using the 2nd and 3rd string for all but the last notes.

Track 52

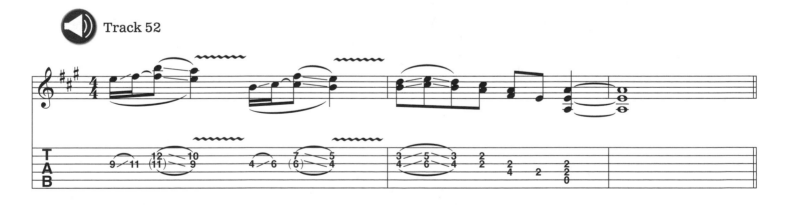

Of course, you don't have to limit yourself to double stops. Experiment with every combination of strings. There are no rules (except Rule Number One and Rule Number Two!).

CHAPTER 10
COUNTRY LICKS THAT ROCK

Growing up in Kentucky, I was exposed to a lot of bluegrass and country music as well as Southern rock bands like the Allman Brothers. Later, I heard Joe Ely's band with Lloyd Maine's overdriven pedal steel guitar. When I joined Ely's band a few years later, I had a chance to really develop my own style, and I drew heavily on all of these influences. Pedal steel–style bends and banjo-style rolls and rakes are techniques you can apply to any style of music.

I've found that a "pick and fingers" right-hand technique works best for most of these licks. When I pop strings, I mainly use my middle finger. Let's look at some basic pedal steel licks in A.

This example is played on the 1st and 2nd strings. Use your middle finger to play the notes on the 1st string (upstrokes) and your pick to play the notes on the 2nd string (downstrokes).

 Track 53 Fast and Slow Versions

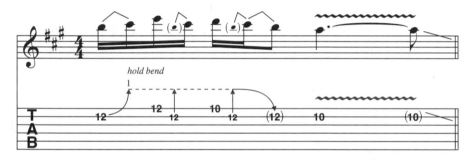

Now let's expand on this idea. This is also played entirely on the 1st and 2nd strings. The lick starts in 10th position, moves to 8th position, and ends up in 3rd position. I prefer to move up and down the fingerboard for these licks. While you can play them without moving around as much (by including the 3rd string), I prefer the feel and tone of bending the 2nd string. Also, I find it easier to visualize where the right notes are when I'm playing a long ascending or descending lick at a fast tempo.

 Track 54 Fast and Slow Versions

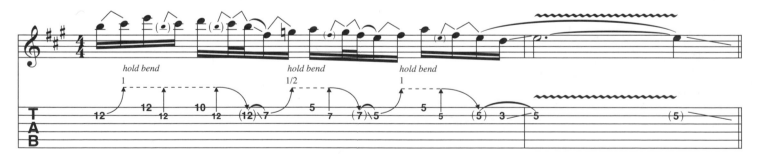

Here is a lick that descends from 12th position all the way down, again in A Mixolydian. Except for the last bar, do all of the bending on the 2nd string with the 3rd finger of your left hand.

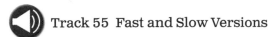

Track 55 Fast and Slow Versions

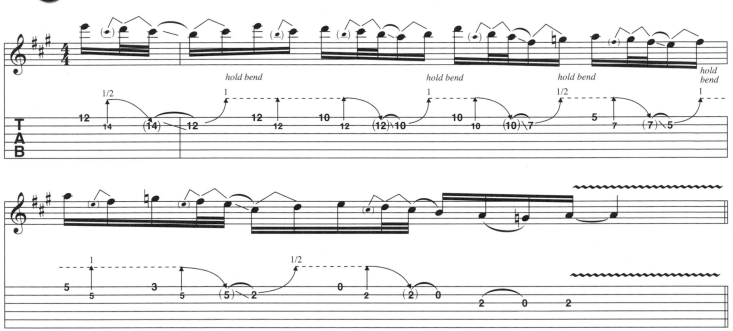

Now let's bring in the 3rd finger and do some three- and four-string licks that combine bending with rakes and rolls. The lick starts with a rake on the top three strings. To rake, drag the pick across the strings with an upstroke. Notice that I start with the 3rd string already bent with my 2nd finger, and I use my right-hand middle finger to pluck all of the notes on the 1st string.

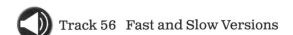

Track 56 Fast and Slow Versions

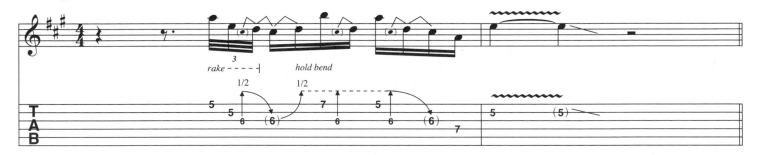

This next example starts with a rake where the first two notes are picked and the third note is played with the middle finger. In this case the C♯ is bent to D with the first finger.

Track 57 Slow and Fast Versions

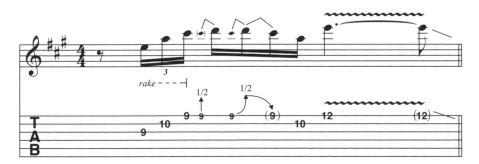

So far, we've played examples that work over an A7 (Mixolydian) chord. Let's take the example from Track 56 and put some rhythm behind it.

 **Track 58**

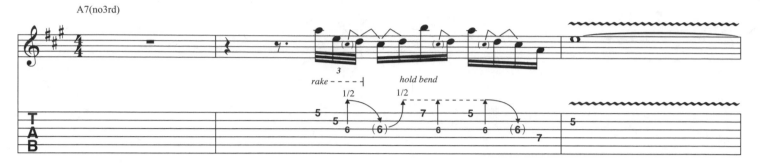

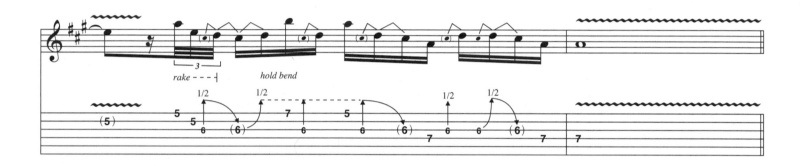

Now, here's the same lick over E7.

 **Track 59**

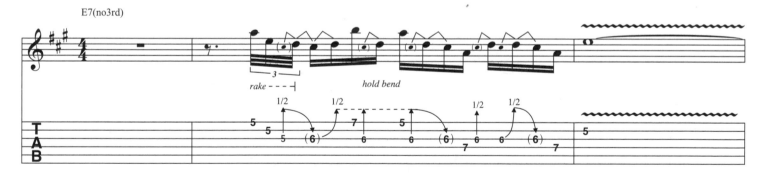

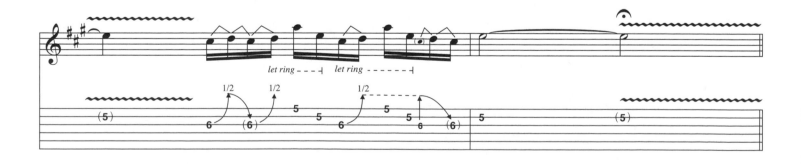

It doesn't sound so country anymore. Remember that A Mixolydian and E Dorian have the same notes as D major (they are the 5th and 2nd modes of D major, respectively), which means you can also play this lick over a D major chord.

Track 60

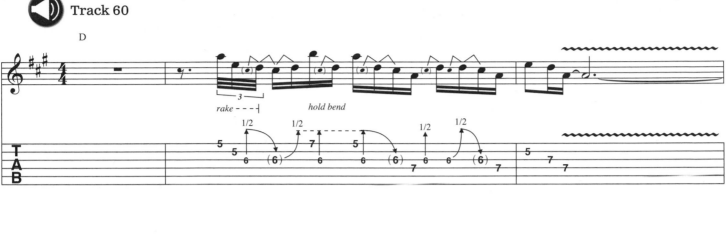

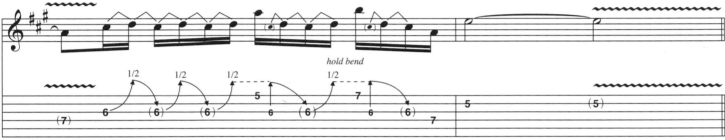

Now let's look at some right-hand rolls. This lick is in D, and I alternate my pick and right-hand middle finger. Note that the top two notes stay the same throughout.

Track 61 Fast and Slow Versions

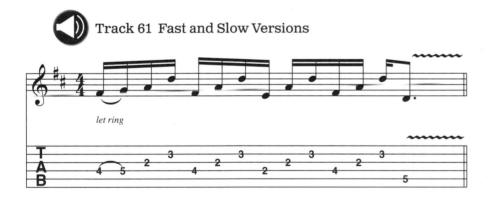

In the next example, I just roll through four different chords (D, C, G, Dadd9). Play the first three notes of each chord with a downstroke rake, and the fourth note of each chord with your middle finger.

Track 62

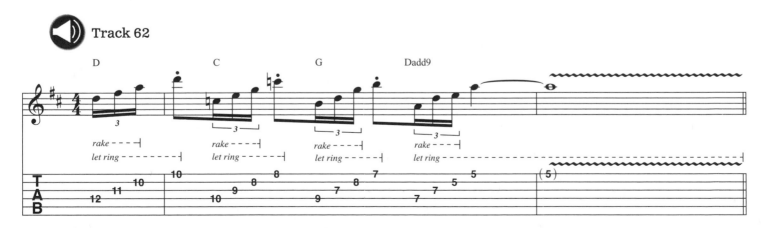

Here is a similar lick an octave lower using the 3rd, 4th, and 5th strings.

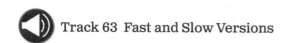

Track 63 Fast and Slow Versions

Now listen to it in a different context. Think outside the box.

Track 64

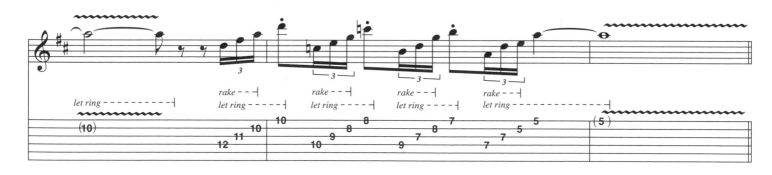

CHAPTER 11
BORROWING FROM JAZZ

When I was 15, my guitar teacher turned me on to jazz guitarist Wes Montgomery. Hearing Wes was like finding a whole new world I never knew existed. Technically, he was playing much more advanced than I was used to hearing, but at the same time he had such depth of feeling—which is what has always drawn me to particular musicians. His phrasing, tone, choice of notes, and command of the guitar knocked me out and inspired me to listen to jazz players on every instrument.

Listening to different styles of music challenges your ear. In general, jazz is harmonically more complex than most rock music. In a typical jazz solo, you might use several different scales. Some tunes require you to use a different scale for every bar. Even if you don't aspire to be an accomplished jazz player, there is much to be gained from listening to jazz and challenging yourself both harmonically and rhythmically.

Let's look at two jazz-influenced licks played over a rock groove. In both of the examples below, I play out of A Mixolydian with some chromatic passing tones thrown in. Any time there is an interval of a whole step (two frets), you can play the note in between as a passing tone. Phrasing-wise, I imply a relaxed swing feel over a pretty rigid groove. I slur some of the notes and play legato in a number of places similar to the way a horn player might phrase the licks.

Track 65

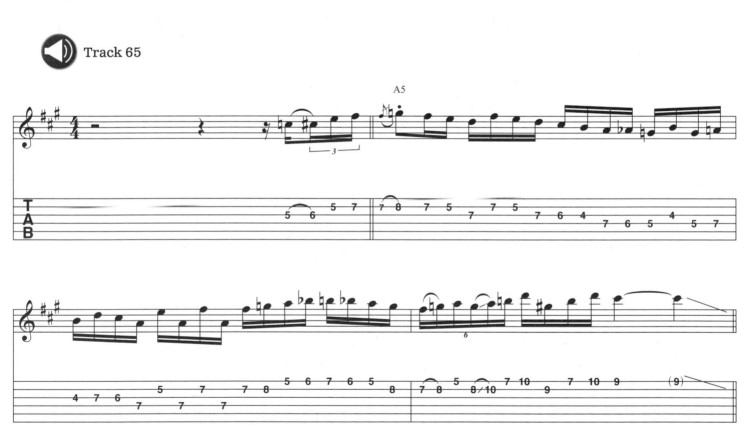

43

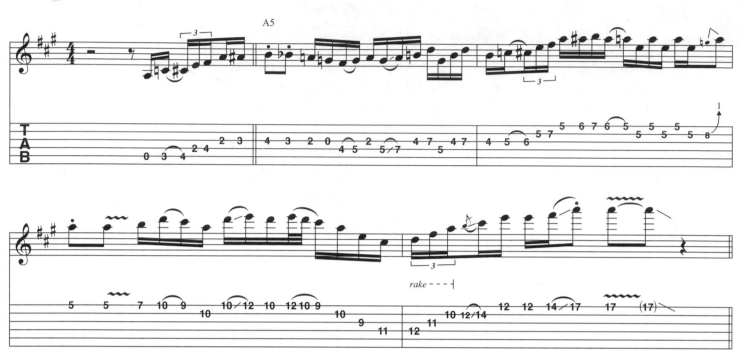

Now let's play in a shuffle feel—again, A Mixolydian with passing tones. Rhythmically, I phrase like a horn player. In the first lick I pop some of the notes. This phrase would sound right at home in a country groove as well. Jazz, country—it's all good. In the last phrase, I fret the A at the 5th fret with my little finger while I walk down the scale, alternating the A with the other notes. I play the A with my right-hand middle finger and pick the descending notes.

 Track 67

If you want to grow as a player, listen to Charlie Parker, John Coltrane, Sonny Rollins, Wes Montgomery, Kenny Burrell, Jim Hall, and as many other jazz greats as you can. Take what you learn from them, blend it in with your other influences, and make it your own. This last music example is a 20-bar solo that combines all of the techniques in this book. Listen and learn.

Track 68

I've added four 12-bar comping tracks so you can get in some practice.

Shuffle in E

 Track 69

Shuffle in A

Track 71

Straight Feel in E

Track 70

Straight Feel in A

Track 72

CHAPTER 12
FINDING YOUR OWN VOICE

When I first started playing guitar, I didn't ever think about having a style or a sound that was my own—I just wanted to learn as much as I could as quickly as possible. I began by imitating—or at least trying to imitate—my favorite players. This was and still is a great way to learn. I really didn't discriminate too much stylistically. Growing up in Kentucky, I was exposed to a wide variety of styles of music, and I realize now that I borrowed liberally from all of them. I listened to Hendrix, Duane Allman, Roy Buchanan, Jeff Beck, and hundreds of other rock players as well as blues players like B.B. King, Albert Collins, Magic Sam, and Albert King. I went to the bluegrass festivals that were held around Louisville. I took lessons from a great teacher who turned me on to Wes Montgomery and many other great jazz players. My father listened to country music so I had that influence at home. I was lucky enough not to have someone telling me that you couldn't take a bluegrass or country lick and play it through a Marshall on "10," or, that you weren't supposed to play funk licks in a shuffle feel. Gradually, all of these influences blended together into a style of my own. I didn't do this consciously—it just happened. By keeping an open mind and listening to a wide variety of music, you are much more likely to come up with your own sound.

When I tried to learn solos from records, I tried to imitate not only the actual licks, but the tone as well. Many times it was really frustrating not to be able to get the same sound or effect as was on the recording. After a while, though, I got better at mimicking what I was hearing. I realized how much of a player's sound is in their hands. I also learned to identify different guitars and amps and started trying to do minor setup work on my own guitar; this really allowed me to get in touch with my instrument. I figured out how I liked my action, what gauge strings worked best for me, and basically how to get the most out of each particular guitar. When it comes to setting up a guitar, everybody likes something a little different. By learning to do basic setups and repairs (teachers and trustworthy gear experts in music shops are good sources for information in this department), you can figure out a lot about what you like and what works best for you. For instance, note that low action is not always better—I've found string bending to be easier and a guitar's tone in general to be fatter when you raise the action. Experiment! With a little patience, you can find out what works best for you.

Whenever you have the opportunity, try out as many different guitars as you can. Note which guitars your favorite players use, try them out, and make up your own mind about what feels and sounds good to you. When I moved to Austin, Texas, in 1983, most of the players in town were playing Stratocasters—which also happened to be the guitar I owned. I decided to look for something different, and when I played a Paul Reed Smith, I knew I had found my guitar. It had a unique look and it definitely didn't sound like a Strat.

Every now and then, someone tells me that they can always spot my playing on the radio or on a CD. It is very gratifying to think that I indeed have a unique sound. Don't be afraid of anything, keep an open mind, and remember that the tone is in your hands. You will find your own voice.

CHAPTER 13
THE IMPORTANCE OF PLAYING LIVE

There aren't many shortcuts when it comes to learning how to play the guitar. You have to put in the time. Having said that, I believe that every hour of live playing (or at least playing with other musicians), is worth seven or eight hours of practice. When I was 16, I met Pat Metheny at one of his shows and I pestered him for all kinds of advice. After being very patient with me, he basically said, "Play gigs—play as many gigs as possible." And, in fact, every major breakthrough in my playing, whether it was related to technique, finding *my* voice, or my approach to soloing, has come during a gig. I've played in country bands, funk bands, blues bands, rock bands, jazz rock bands, and a lot of bands you wouldn't want to know about. I've played thousands of gigs, some of which were among the greatest experiences of my life, some I'd just as soon not remember—but I guarantee you, I learned something worthwhile on every one of them.

Even if you just get together to jam with friends, I encourage you to make the most of any opportunity to play with other people and/or in front of an audience. There is something intangible about being on the spot (or in the moment) that allows you to focus in a way you can't when practicing alone.

Doing studio work is in some ways totally different than playing live. Live, I play physically harder and I'm more concerned about playing emotionally and in the moment than I am about technical precision. If you are going to do studio sessions and expect to get called back, you must be able to play in tune, have great time, and have a great tone. Often, the emphasis is on coming up with a great part on the spot and playing it perfectly the first time. I love playing live and recording, and over the years I've tried to blur the lines between how I approach each situation. I try to bring the fire of playing live into the studio. The things I've learned playing live, and especially playing in a band, are invaluable in the studio as well.

Playing in a band will not only help you to develop as a soloist, but will improve your rhythm playing as well. If you want to take your playing to the next level, get out and play some gigs!